I0825231
California
Louisiana
North Dakota
Nevada
Delaware
Oregon
Vermont
North Carolina
Illinois
Connecticut
Virginia
Alabama
Alaska
South Carolina
Massachusetts
Maine
Maryland
Florida
Indiana
Iowa
Colorado
Montana
Minnesota
Wyoming
Washington
Hawaii

Random House Books for Young Readers
An imprint of Random House Children's Books
A division of Penguin Random House LLC
1745 Broadway, New York, NY 10019
penguinrandomhouse.com
Seussville.com
rhcbooks.com

Hand Lettering: Amit E. Sethi | Editor: Cat Reynolds | Designer: Marianna Smirnova | Copy Editor: Stephanie Bay
Managing Editor: Julie Gayle | Production Manager: Amy Bowman

Library of Congress Cataloging-in-Publication Data is available upon request.
ISBN 979-8-217-22856-0 (trade) — ISBN 979-8-217-22857-7 (lib. bdg.) — ISBN 979-8-217-22858-4 (ebook)

Manufactured in China
10 9 8 7 6 5 4 3 2 1

The authorized representative in the EU for product safety and compliance is Penguin Random House Ireland, Morrison Chambers, 32 Nassau Street, Dublin D02 YH68, Ireland, https://eu-contact.penguin.ie.

Random House Children's Books supports the First Amendment and celebrates the right to read.

Sing the 50 United States!

By Dr. Seuss

illustrated by Tom Brannon

Random House New York

To sing the 50 United States
you have to use your brain.

Massachusetts.
Minnesota.
Missouri and Montana.
M-i-s-s-Mississippi.
Maryland!
Michigan and Maine!

Minnesota
Michigan
Michigan
Maine
Missouri
Mississippi
Maryland

To sing the 50 United States
is a big job for the mouth.
Virginia!
West Virginia!
Don't forget the two **Dakotas!**
And a couple of **Carolinas**
which are likewise **North** and **South.**

Minnesota
Michigan
Michigan
Maine
West Virginia
Virginia
Maryland
Missouri
Mississippi

And . . . and . . .

Maine
Michigan
Michigan
Massachusetts
Maryland
West Virginia
Virginia
North Carolina
South Carolina
Missouri
Mississippi
Idaho

Idaho . . . ?

Yes, **Idaho!**
And **O-HI-O!**
Come on! Let's go!

New Jersey.
New York.
New Hampshire.
And New MEX-I-CO!
Phew!
New Mexico
New Hampshire
New Jersey
New York

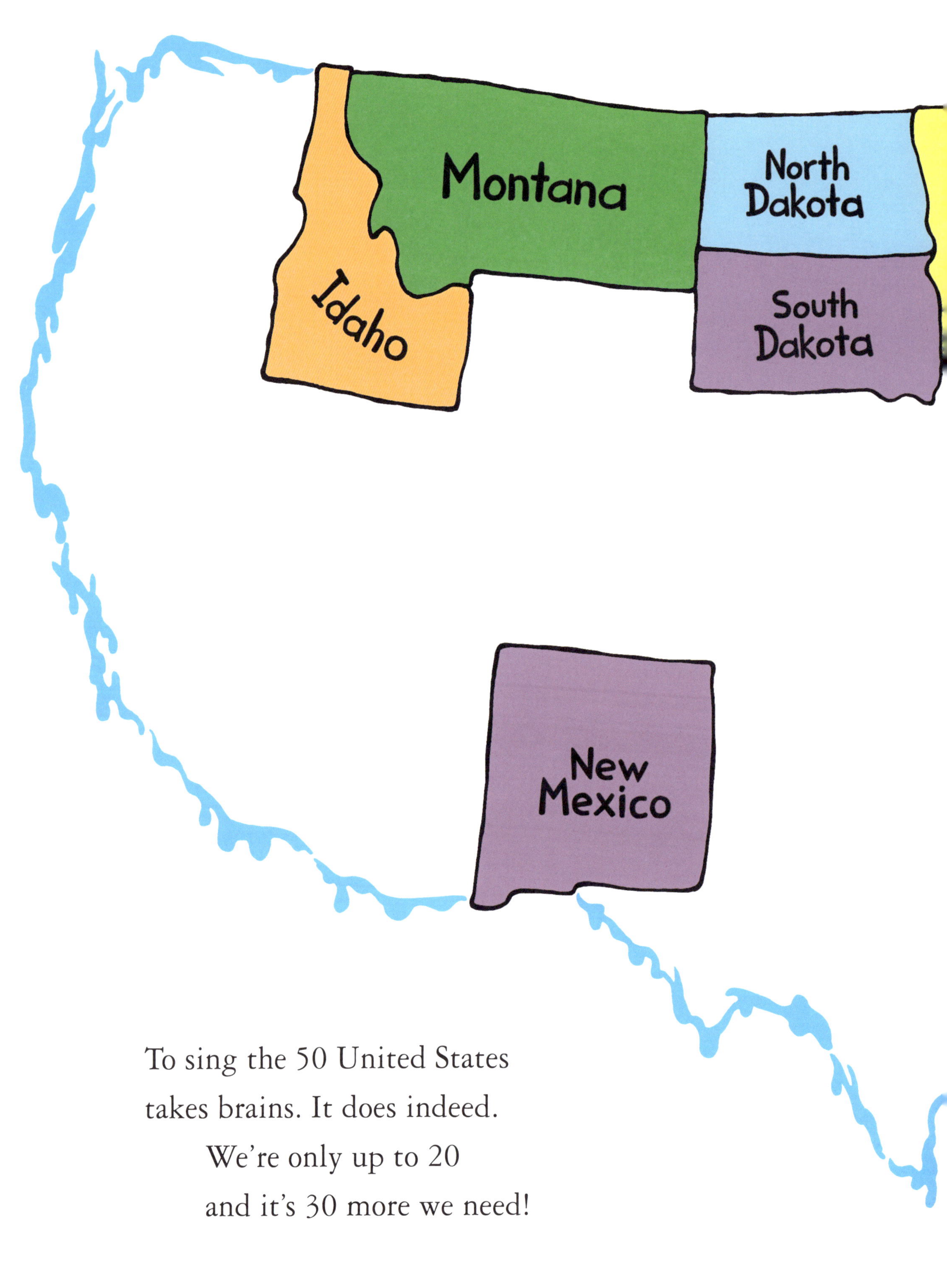

To sing the 50 United States
takes brains. It does indeed.
We're only up to 20
and it's 30 more we need!

Michigan
Michigan
Maine
New Hampshire
New York
Massachusetts
New Jersey
Ohio
West Virginia
Maryland
Virginia
Missouri
North Carolina
South Carolina
Mississippi

May I bring up Nebraska?
Nebraska

Yeah! And how about **Alaska**?
And those two that begin with "T."
T-T-T-T-TEXAS!
TENNESSEE!

You're up to 24 now.

You might make it if you're lucky.

Rhode Island!

Oregon!

Pennsylvania!

Kansas and **Kentucky!**

Pennsylvania
Kansas
Kentucky

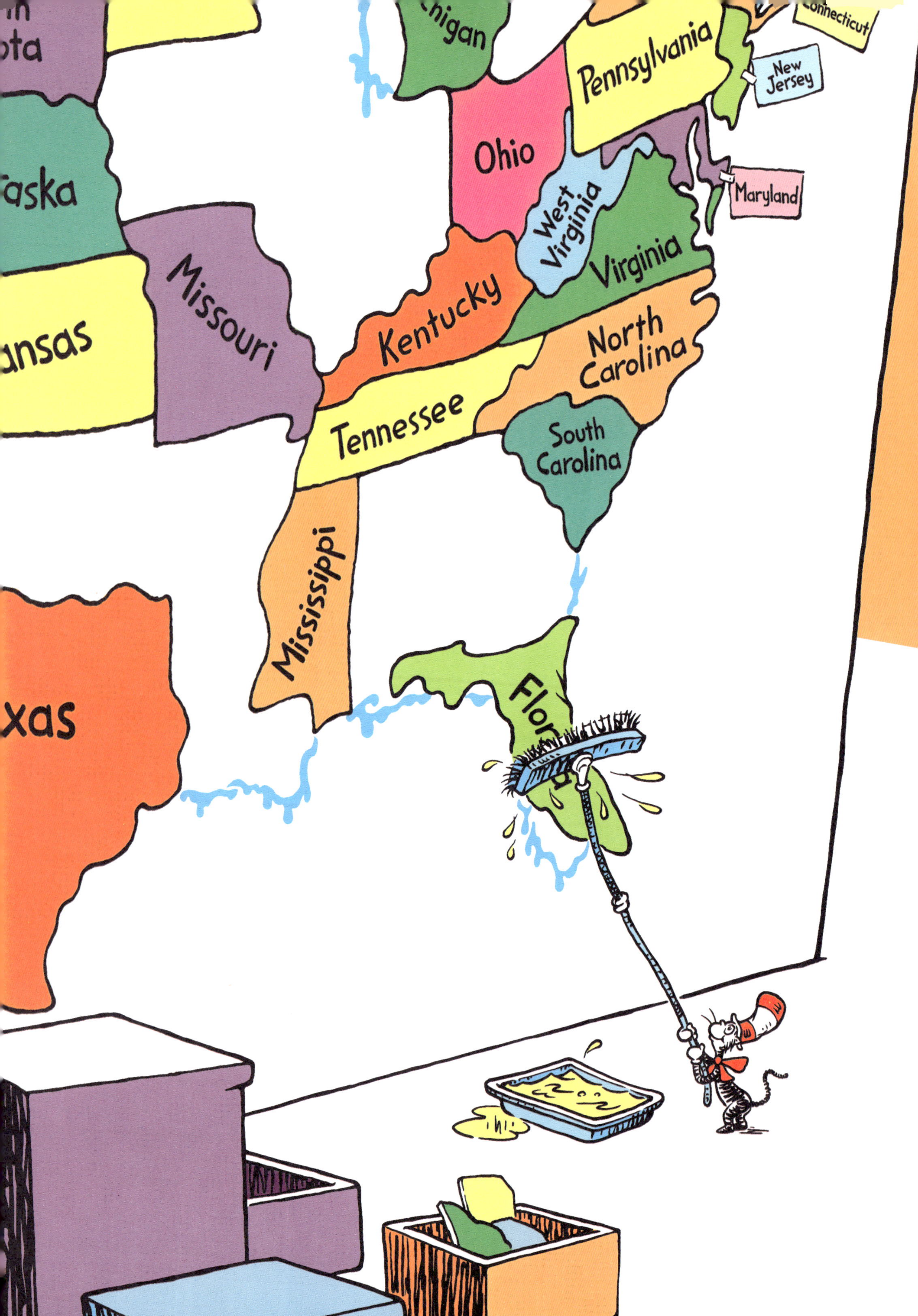
Connecticut
Pennsylvania
New Jersey
Ohio
Maryland
West Virginia
Virginia
Missouri
Kentucky
North Carolina
Tennessee
South Carolina
Mississippi

Iowa.
Georgia.
Florida. And Del-a-ware!
Alabama!
Arkansas!
Arizona . . . !
And where do you go from there?

Illinois . . . ?

OH, BOY!!

To sing the 50 United States
you mustn't get in a rut.
California.
Colorado.
And **Con-nect-i-cut!**
Vermont . . . Indiana!
Utah . . . Louisiana!

California

Wyoming!
Wisconsin!
WASH-ING-TON!
And NEVADA! And HAWAII!

And that's 50! **AND WE'RE DONE!**

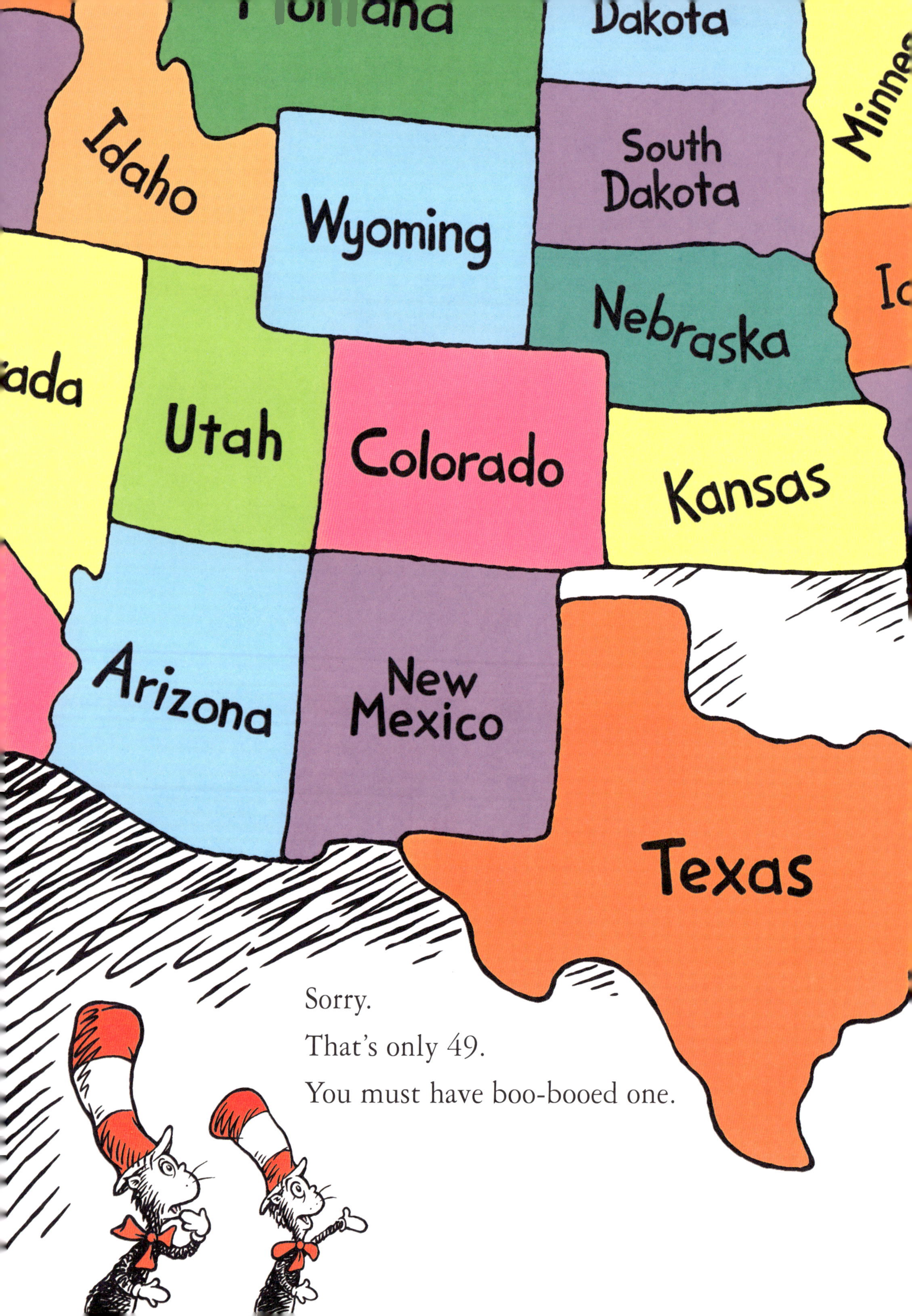

Sorry.

That's only 49.

You must have boo-booed one.

Michigan
Wisconsin
Michigan
Vermont
New York
Rhode Island
Connecticut
Pennsylvania
New Jersey
Illinois
Indiana
Ohio
West Virginia
Delaware
Maryland
Virginia
Kentucky
North Carolina
Tennessee
South Carolina
Mississippi
Alabama
Georgia
Louisiana

Oh no!

Oh . . . ohhh!
Oh . . . OH!

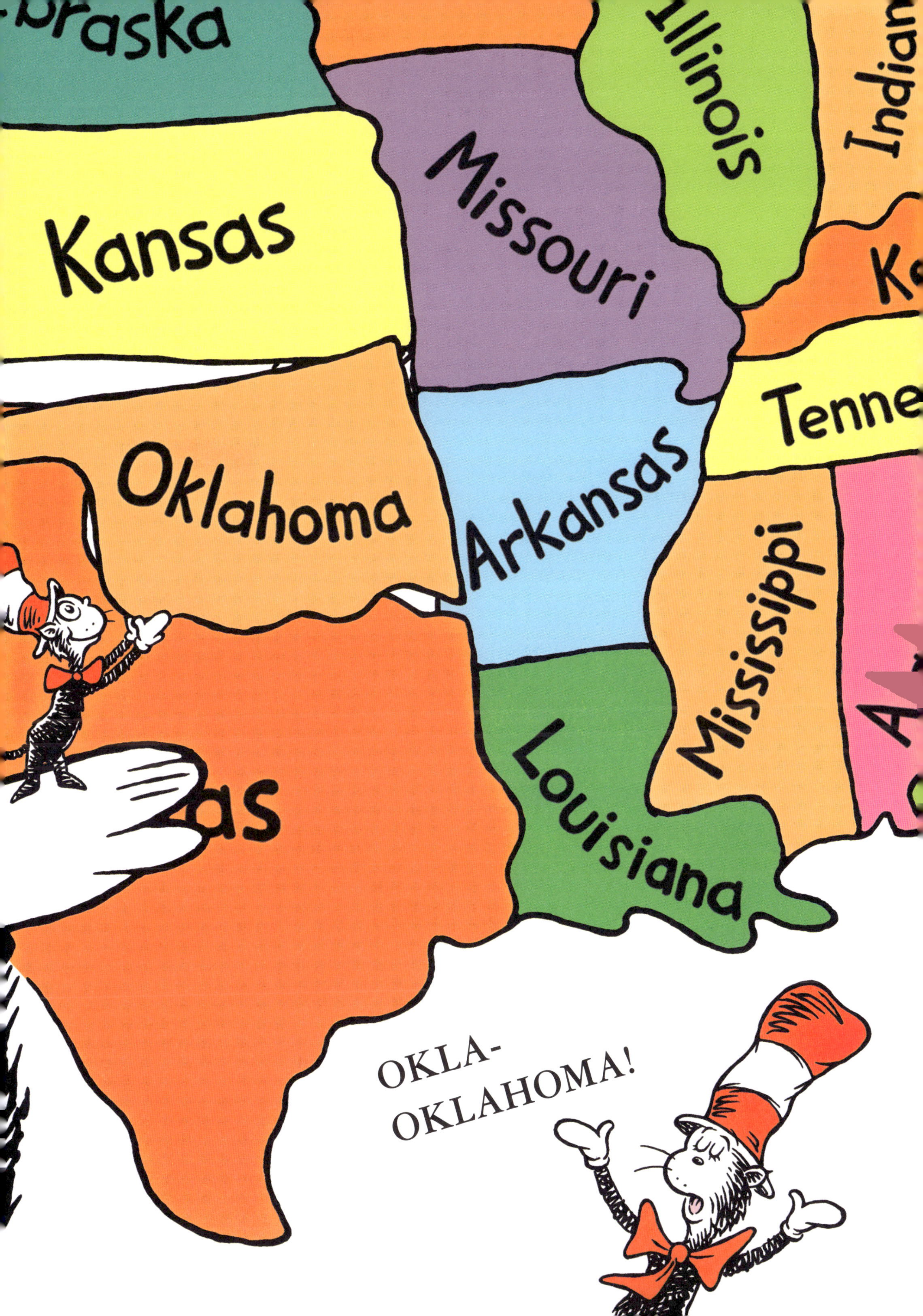
Kansas
Missouri
Illinois
Oklahoma
Arkansas
Mississippi
Louisiana
OKLA-
OKLAHOMA!

We can sing the 50 United States.
We told you from the start.
To sing the 50 United States . . .
you sing them from your heart!

Minnesota
Michigan
Wisconsin
Michigan
Maine
Vermont
New Hampshire
New York
Massachusetts
Rhode Island
Connecticut
Pennsylvania
New Jersey
Delaware
Maryland
Iowa
Illinois
Indiana
Ohio
West Virginia
Virginia
Kansas
Missouri
Kentucky
North Carolina
Tennessee
Oklahoma
Arkansas
South Carolina
Mississippi
Alabama
Georgia
Louisiana
Florida

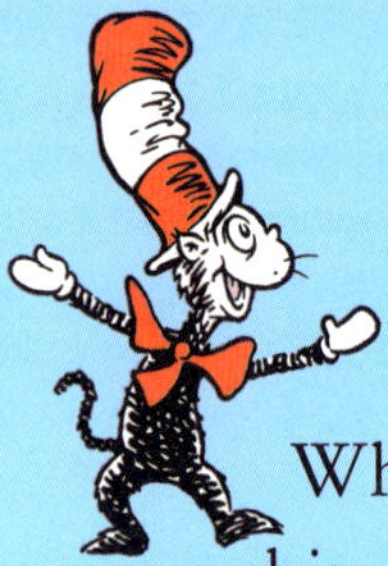

A NOTE FROM THE PUBLISHER

What do you picture when you hear the words *buried treasure*? Gold coins in a ship at the bottom of the ocean? A chest full of jewels, underneath a red *X*?

How about an unsuspecting box in a library? Because that's just where the treasure you hold in your hands was found—in the archives of the Dr. Seuss Collection at the University of California San Diego's Geisel Library (so called after Dr. Seuss's real name, Theodor Seuss Geisel).

There are over 20,000 items in the Dr. Seuss Collection. Little did anyone know, however, that among them was a never-before-seen project left unfinished by Ted Geisel: *Sing the 50 United States!* Discovered in May 2025, just over one year before the country's 250th birthday, it was a gift waiting to be opened!

Several boxes held variations of the same song with the title *Sing the 50 United States!* Below, you can see the evolution of the work: from the early stages of a first draft handwritten by Ted Geisel on notebook paper to a finalized typeset manuscript.

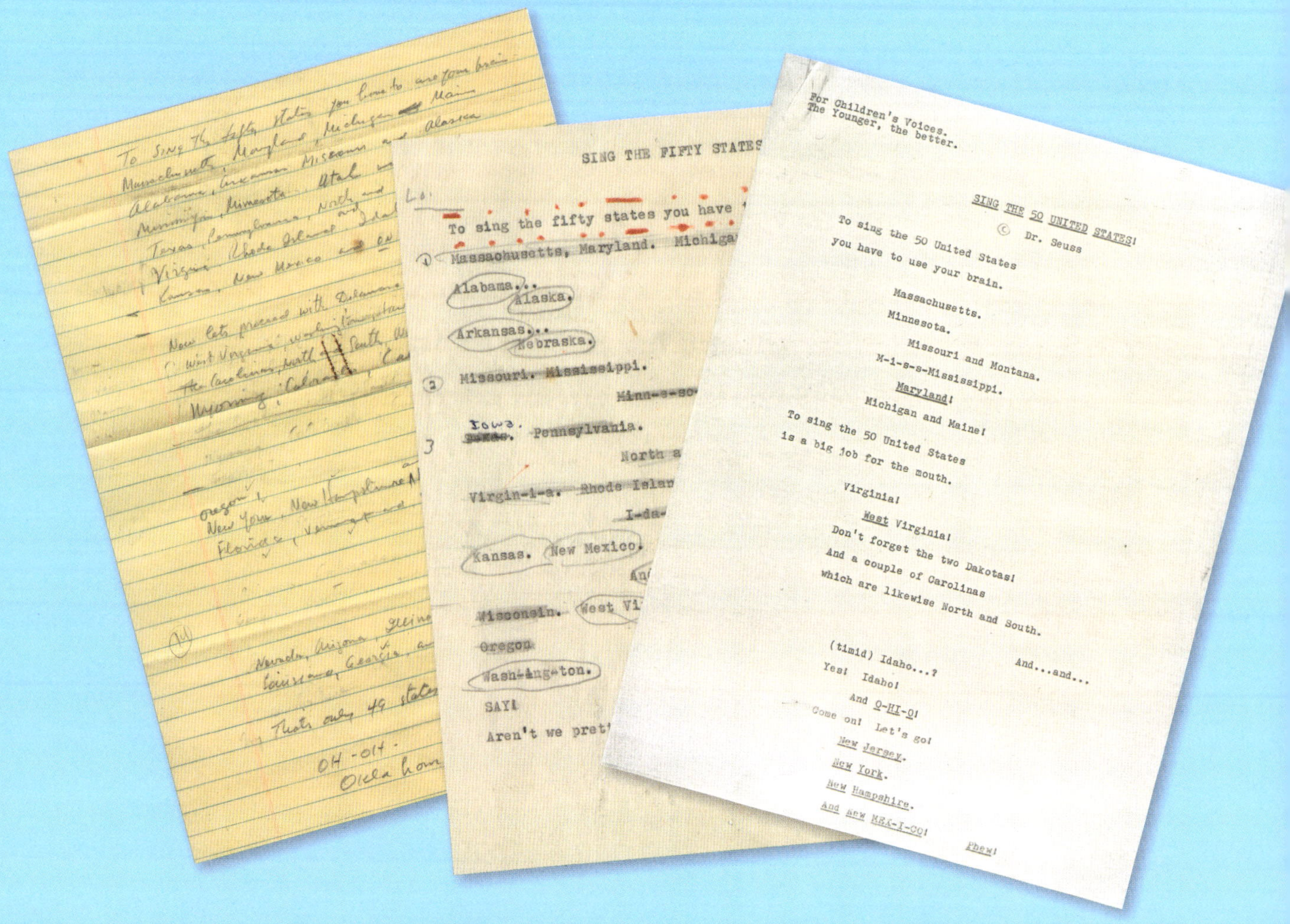

For Children's Voices.
The Younger, the better.

SING THE 50 UNITED STATES!
© Dr. Seuss

To sing the 50 United States
you have to use your brain.

Massachusetts.
Minnesota.
Missouri and Montana.
M-i-s-s-Mississippi.
Maryland!
Michigan and Maine!

To sing the 50 United States
is a big job for the mouth.

Virginia!
West Virginia!
Don't forget the two Dakotas!
And a couple of Carolinas
which are likewise North and South.

(timid) Idaho...? And...and...
Yes! Idaho!
And O-HI-O!
Come on! Let's go!
New Jersey.
New York.
New Hampshire.
And new MEX-I-CO! Phew!